POEMS TO THE HEART

POEMS TO THE HEART

THOUGHTS ON VALUES AND LIFE'S EXPERIENCES

Barry Faith

ISBN: 978 09522003 21

https://www.heart-poems.com

Published by Barry Faith

Cover design: Paul Jones.

Typography and copyediting: Words into Type
http://wordsintotype.ssbarnhill.com/

WARNING

The poem 'Pro vanity' is about vulgarity and so contains vulgar words.

WHY MY POETRY?

You'll find some good,
   maybe find some crappy.
Just treasure those that you relate to,
   make you thoughtful—and maybe happy!

What's your
mood?

Heart map

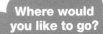

Where would you like to go?

Where is your heart today?

CONTENTS

BEHAVIOUR

CONFLICT

SURVIVAL

PHILOSOPHY

LANGUAGE

PLACES

ENVIRONMENT

PUBLIC SERVICE CORRUPTION

THE REST

Contents

POSTSCRIPT

INTRODUCTION
WHAT OTHERS SAY…

Excellent, perceptive poems with real pace.

Matthew Syed – Multi-award–winning journalist for *The Times*; television and radio contributor; author on high-performance mindset and children's books. Table tennis champion and Olympics competitor.

Barry's poetry relates to things that matter in people's lives and the sentiments expressed mirror feelings that many people struggle to put into words.

John Jenkins – author, editor, and publisher of 45 books; former night editor of the *Daily Telegraph*.

Barry Faith's poems are wide-ranging in their subject-matter, from war to marriage, people and their behaviour, politics and the environment, with moods from humour and thoughtfulness to sadness and tragedy. They are remarkable for their vivid imagery, colour and sense of rhythm, catching the nuances of contrary emotions with a keen awareness of the contradictions of life.

Roger Turner – author of five nonfiction books and several volumes of poetry, including *The Hippo*.

It's curious. We read a well-written text about some aspect of life and find it interesting, even memorable. However…

Take that same message and convert it into good poetry and suddenly the text carries more weight. It becomes truly thought-provoking, worthy of our time. And the very act of contemplating feels good, part of our 'mindfullness' in the modern parlance.

The poet has striven to find the exact turn of phrase that is short on words, long on meaning. The poet's skill has somehow imbued the poem with an extra power to penetrate our mind and touch our heart, maybe even change us for the better.

That's what I experience when I read Barry Faith's poems and I expect you will too.

Stuart Wyatt – author

*In science, one tries to tell
people, in such a way as to be
understood by everyone,
something that no one ever
knew before. But in poetry,
it's the exact opposite.*

Paul Dirac OM FRS
English physicist and compatriot of Albert Einstein

THANKS AND SOURCES

The poems I have written could not have occurred without my life experiences and the inspiration I have received from some great poets and songwriters. These include Rudyard Kipling, Denis Waitley, Albert Hammond, and many others. The titles that I mention of these great artists and thinkers can be found and read on the internet.

I have used various sources, such as wiki, for the supporting material about such predecessors and encourage you to research their various personalities. Their backgrounds are diverse and insightful, and their achievements are humbling to us lesser mortals.

Thanks to those family and friends who have helped me in some way to reach this point of publication.

APPROACH AND EXPLANATIONS

The poems are placed in specific categories and, while it is arguable that some could be grouped differently, do not let this spoil your enjoyment!

Some poems have explanations about their genesis and others do not. In most cases, explanations are on the left pages with their poems starting on the facing right-hand page.

Make this book a part of your life journey

Consider further enhancing your reading experience by adding your thoughts to the poems you like, and their explanations.

♡♡♡

Poetry says something that has never been said before and describes a reality previously hidden from us.

Unattributable

POEMS TO THE HEART

PREAMBLE

Upon watching a television drama when the actor used the phrase, 'To leave behind a thing of beauty', I reflected on the profoundness of that phrase.

The Greek statesman Pericles put this into a nutshell: 'What you leave behind is not what is engraved in stone monuments, but what is woven into the lives of others.'

Only those who follow me on life's journey can decide what I leave behind and so posterity will be the judge of the value of my poetry.

LEAVING SOMETHING BEHIND

On our way to who knows where,
To a place with no cares,
What is now on my mind,
Is choosing what to leave behind.

Should it be the wealth accrued?
To help our offspring with their brood?
And future kin yet to come?
Safety net when hope is done?

Should it be the paths I've trod?
The ups and downs, the unturned sods?
Should it be those steps I've taken,
To live for values not forsaken?

Should it be the loves and lives?
That human mix we all desire?
How about the values lived?
Not too many to be forgiven!

The ins and outs, the in-betweens,
The paths forsaken, never seen.
A route map of my lifelong journey,
Many paths but seldom turning.

Is my poetry best to leave,
To help others when they grieve?

The words that tumble from my mind,
Making sense — for those left behind.
How best for me to tell the tale?
Forever fresh — never stale.

What can I leave for others to find?
When in despair they search their minds?
For thoughts and deeds that for ever shine;
For them, in turn, to leave behind.

September 2018

Preamble

POETRY THOUGHTS

After many years of writing poems, I decided to publish. I found out that the best way to get a poetry publisher interested is to win poetry competitions.

I started researching the poetry market by subscribing to the *Spectator* (which publishes poems) and joining the Poetry Society and researching its poetry competitions and their winners. I also researched the winners of the prestigious 'Bridport Prize' competition.

I found that many of the winners' poems were 'deep' to the point of incomprehension for my simple mind and so lost interest in reading them. It seemed to me that, to win such competitions, one had to be schooled in the intricacies of the established poetry schools of thought.

My liking is for poets such as Rudyard Kipling who, if you discount the current view of his jingoistic and empire-focussed writings, wrote simple and straightforward verse. Kipling was the 'working (wo)man's poet'.

Poems that are for you and me,
Are not what they are meant to be.
Poetry that should be so fine,
With those very careful metred lines.
So say the great and good of the stanzas,
Crafted by and for — those specialist —
    poetic — dancers.
To the tune of what should be
In polite poetic society.

Let's write instead for humble masses,
With limited prose and rhyming verses.
Let us give them works so fine,
So they can understand each line.
Poetry can be the finest art,
When written for the proletariat.
Let these words fly from my mind —
For the broader tastes of mankind.

March 2019

PEOPLE

This category is about relationships, relations, friends, and colleagues.

Just as snowflakes are formed by their unique paths on their journey from clouds to the earth, so are all of us uniquely formed by our individual set of experiences during our life journey.

INSPIRATION

BILLY JOEL

For me, this is reflected in the characters in Billy Joel's song *Piano Man*, which I never tire of.

Just as people meet socially in pubs and bars, so also do we meet in workplaces, coming together for a time and then departing to go our separate ways.

DENIS WAITLEY

Many years ago I listened to Denis Waitley's teaching audio *The Seeds of Greatness* several times while driving around the UK and was profoundly affected by the good sense and myriad tips Denis offered. These have helped me lead a more fulfilling and productive career and life.

Dr Waitley's poem *Take A Moment* encapsulates, for me, our vitally important role of nurturing our relationships, especially with our children, for they are the source of the generations to come.

APOLOGY

Apologies (or congratulations?) to those relations
and friends (living or dead) I have not yet written
a poem about!

♡♡♡

To those I have forgotten or not yet put to rhyme,
To you, I dedicate some future time.
When that will be? Who knows when?
Maybe tomorrow or perhaps later then.

To reflect your ways and your living,
Though poetic licence may mean —
   I will need forgiving.
As facts are changed to make it rhyme,
Admission will follow with which you'll chime.

It may depend on inspiration or deadline,
Whichever way it will be just fine.

August 2015

HELPING

A strong purpose in my life is investment in the future, and a key part of that is to have values that are passed down the generations

♡♡♡

Helping with our family
Is the way I want to be.
Helping them to build and grow,
Helping us to reap and sow.

With each passing generation
So we build our family nation,
Parent to child and so on
Long time after I am gone.

So set the ethos, live the creed,
Create the thoughts, do the deed.
Build for those yet to be born,
To that end let us all be sworn.

April 2014

SALAD DAYS

The 1980s – these were golden years; when my parents were recently retired.

Dad made their garden bloom and Mum excelled at filling our plates with delicious salad from his gardening efforts when we visited them.

Such treasured moments are extremely vivid and remain with me.

♡♡♡

Spring onions from Dad's garden,
Ham from Tom's corner shop.
Mum's Jersey boiled potatoes,
Salad days — with cream atop.

Round table set for many,
Filled from edge to edge;
With fare, condiments, and cutlery,
And our individual pledge.

To enjoy both food and kinship;
To swap tales and jokes and more;
To imbibe in the house of Mum & Dad;
And then finish off with chores.

With Tash & Jess, our children,
With Maureen — wife — and me.
With Jack & Maisie — parents,
With all of us to see

A family together,
On a sunny summer day.
No cares apart our plates to clear,
And then outside to play.

Salad days are what I remember.

2009

DAD

John Albert Faith
15th March 1915 – 11th November 1997

We all have memories of our parents and their
impact on our lives.

It took me over five years after his death in 1997
to write this poem for Dad. I needed to do it
before I visited his grave for the first time after
the burial of his ashes.

♡♡♡

Do you remember the toy milk float, Dad,
  which you and Mum had bought?
I fell down the stairs that birthday,
  in anticipation I thought.

Then there was the model railway,
  you made with patience and with skill,
I discovered you assembling rails,
  brass wire… now that was a thrill!

No money in your pocket,
  just hands and mind to find,
The answers to a small boy's Christmas wish,
  you dedicated time.

The clock was just a passing phase
  as I learned and built my skills.
You came home and nary a word was said,
With cogs and springs by me were spread…
I had no answer to how they had fitted well.

You let me build a treetop house,
  an adventure few have had.
From here I viewed to distant lands, strengthened
  mind and body – thanks for that, my Dad.

The shed was all I could ask for,
  an appendage to your own,
Where I could spend countless hours,
  with model engines —
           — and their ceaseless drone.

The practical side of life now neared,
  as time came to earn my way.
You helped me learn the money side,
  my bike — partly — you made me pay.

Too soon I left for my career,
  from home a sad farewell,
To return periodically, with stories to tell.
And on my twenty-first, a present you did buy
Gold cuff links, a life gift, to recall you by.

In later years you helped me —
   an extension to our home,
With skills you'd learned over many years,
   now so finely honed.

All four and seventy years now told,
   but still, you laboured on,
Putting me right, without pretension,
   my wiring was soon done.

It's all over now, Dad,
   it's my turn to show my kids the way.
To help them to build and grow,
   to face each and every day.

You showed me how to do it, Dad,
   though you may have never realised how,
And so it's too late to tell you, Dad,
   how much you made my now.

Thanks for all you've given me —
   more than you'll ever know
In parentage, we sow the seeds
   from which our children's children grow.

February 2002

People

MUM

Maisie Faith
5th May 1919 – 7th June 2002

Mum was a very gentle, happy-go-lucky person, always ready to listen to her family and friends.

Writing my poem about Dad made it easier to write this one in time for Mum's funeral.

To celebrate a life in midst of all the tears,
'Tis a paradox we all face
    with our other hopes and fears.

Dear Mum, now it's tears for you
    and celebration too;
A life fully lived, that we all loved,
    in eighty-one years plus two.

Mother of four, grandmother of more,
    you did your lot for mankind.
So now you'll rest and it's up to us
    to keep your memory in mind.

Kindness and patience were ever your hand,
  played whenever required;
Your smile and your warmth,
  given so freely, meant so much to us…
  An amber glow from a warm-hearted fire.

Now the fire has gone, the stout heart beats no
  more, it's time to lay you to rest.
But the glow lingers on, in our memories so fond,
Mum you really were one of the best!

June 2002

DOROTHY

Dorothy Loughran
21ˢᵗ September 1917 – 24ᵗʰ November 1998

My grandmother, Emily Tomlinson, had nine
children; six survived. Mum and her sister
Dorothy were special chums owing to their
closeness in age. Dorothy's poems inspired me to
write mine.

Dorothy and her husband, Barrel (his nickname),
lived at Oliver's Battery, near Winchester,
Hampshire. When I visited them with Mum,
Dorothy told me about the well in their garden,
from which Oliver Cromwell is said to
have drunk.

Dorothy reminded Mum about the parrot that
their dad, George Tomlinson, brought back from
one of his sea journeys; how their mum, Emily,
didn't like it at first but became very fond of it. It
escaped and Reg (their brother) recaptured it by
getting Dorothy to mimic its 'voice'.

The parrot was stuffed and put on display in
Emily and George's home after it died.

♡♡♡

With words you made your life;
With words, you made your love.
To words you gave your life;
To words, you gave so much.

Communication and imagination
  were your strengths,
And your determination ensured
  you went the length.
Your humour sustained us all,
  and in our minds, you'll still walk tall;
Thro' your words you will live on,
  'till the end of time is done.

Corny lines, but heartfelt

1998

REG

Reginald Tomlinson
18ᵗʰ February 1916 to February 2000

Reg was a dear uncle and friend. Perhaps
everyone has a favourite uncle or aunt. It's all in
the poem.

As an uncle you were kind,
  as an uncle you were good;
As friends, we had our laughs,
  as all friends should.

We spoke about all matters,
  ranging great and small;
We solved some worldly problems;
  however, not them all!

With theories and abstractions,
  we battled with our minds,
From rotary engines thro' relativity,
  we occupied our time.

To reach some odd solution
  that someday may see light,
We searched our old grey matter
  for things outside our sight.

So now you have departed —
  maybe for other kinds
Of mental exercise —
  with other likened minds.

Reg, we will all miss you
  and your unique and special ways.
However, we'll all remember you
  for those not forgotten days.

February 2000

CONTINUITY

Upon hearing of the end of a relative's marriage.

Although such events can cause grief to the involved parties, the children of a union still carry on the bloodline and family ethos.

A piece of our family died today;
Though everyone's here, it has passed away.

Though mother is to daughter
   and father is to son,
A little bit has gone, even though we are still one.

Past the anger and tears, the sorrow and strife,
The part that has died has led to new life.

Kith and kin torn asunder,
   our differences laid bare,
Our bloodlines still run on,
   with our children to share.

Our sons and our daughters
   will continue with our line;
It is through them our unions will eternally shine.

A piece of our family died today,
Though everyone's here, it passed away.

Although it is sad and although there are tears,
Through our children, there is hope,
   which will conquer through the years.

2011

MARRIAGE

I married Maureen in 1976, and our 2015 wedding anniversary caused me to reflect on the undulations of marriage from the pessimistic and optimistic viewpoints.

Marriage with its ups and downs
Brings with it both — smiles and frowns.

But is it up, or the down,
Which brings that smile or that frown?

Some say the word is compromise,
Neither up nor down, a level path —
   are you alive?

An uphill struggle needs mental force;
A downhill slide may end in divorce.

Or is the climbing with achievement?
Until we pass with much bereavement?

And downhill being an easy route?
Peace and quiet for those astute?

Does a level path bring contentment?
No place for mutual resentment?

Whichever path that we choose,
We decide a win or lose.

One thing helps though to be sure,
Right-mate choice is half the cure!

2015

EAVE ENDS

Stuart Wyatt — a good friend, serial entrepreneur, management author, and astute photographer — started his career as a boatbuilder.

His skills and capabilities came to the fore when new eave ends were needed for my daughter Jess's first house in Poole.

The image and so the character of the 100-year-old property, which is embedded in the brickwork, the shape and structure, and the style of items such as the eave ends, has been preserved by Stuart's woodworking master-craftsmanship.

Thanks for the craftsmanship
  and dedication to the task.
You've done everything and more
  than a friend could ask.

Fashioned from the timber
  with knowledge, tools, and know-how,
Into fine-looking eave ends
  which on the building will show how —

In the years to come,
  a master can fashion to the shape,
So the house preserves its character
  and so to its past escape.

September 2014

DAVE

Dave Carey and I met in 1990 whilst volunteering to help the Wessex branch of the Institute of Management. Together, we successfully increased attendance by 80 people per event.

Our friendship continues, along with a common interest in technology and physics and our ability to counsel and mentor each other.

I wanted to give Dave something memorable for his sixtieth birthday in September 2014 and a muse about our friendship seemed a good idea.

♡♡♡

To write a birthday poem
  has proved to be a challenge,
For my friend Dave Carey,
  but one I've surely managed.

For 24 years I've known Dave,
  years of giving and of sharing,
With my good friend Dave,
  years of mutual caring.

Sharing our ideas and thoughts,
  of man, machines, and many things;
Caring through our common values,
  the bells of friendship ring.

The bond of trust is rare,
   and means a lot to me;
The frankness of a kinship,
   to speak, but to let it be.

So when I sound pissed off, Dave,
   don't let this be a worry,
I probably drank too much last night,
   and am still eliminating curry…

A true friend is a rarity,
   something to feed and grow,
To nurture over time,
   to let the friendship flow.

Now from your sixtieth birthday,
   you enter your seventh decade,
A time to do what you've left undone,
   whilst still earning through your trade.

Happy birthday Dave,
   and more of them to come
I look to celebrate your eighty-fourth
   if we can still work out the vector sum!

September 2014

PHIL

Sholing's answer to Lowry
Phil McMahone
25th December 1947 – 14th December 2000

My lasting memory of Phil's talent is the drawing he crafted in Miss Trim's class at St Monica School, Sholing, Southampton, where we grew up.

The drawing was a crowd of people skating and playing on a frozen pond. The detail was astounding, and there were a variety of people in the drawing, doing all sorts of things. I guess this showed an innate ability to observe and comment on human activity.

Phil worked in the insurance business and sold me an endowment policy which paid off handsomely 30-odd years later.

♡♡♡

Forty years of memories, fifty-odd years of life,
The time passes oh so quickly, 'twas just
    yesterday when all was active fun.
From match stick men at St Monica's, through
    bike rides and dusty carts,
        on road and cut and field,
The four of us played and jousted, and camped
    and drank, it seemed always, in the sun.

How soon that time was ended,
  how soon memories took their place,
How soon we all departed
  to join that long rat race.
And so onwards to another journey,
  to places, none of us left can know,
You're pioneering for us Phil,
  the way we all must go!

Thanks for the times together,
  thanks for the policy too—
My plans are soundly based
  with finance – advised by you!
There's nothing left to say now,
  just feelings for a friend who's gone,
Your artistry will be my memory,
  your matchstick men linger on...

December 2000

TOM

Upon hearing of the death of Tom Wellard, in
May 2013, age 66 years.

Tom was a fellow REME* traveller at 36 Heavy
Air Defence Regiment circa 1971–1974.

*The Royal Electrical and Mechanical Engineers.
The technical corps of the British Army,
responsible for the maintenance of equipment
used by the 'teeth arms' (i.e. the fighting soldiers).

Our ageing vulnerability,
Only comes to light when I hear or see,
A friend or colleague's recent passing,
Reminds me of life, non-everlasting.

The end will come to us all,
None can escape the final call;
What stays with those who are left,
Are memories, words and pictures kept.

To late departures and those yet to go,
A farewell now will mean you know,
A cheery goodbye with thoughts in mind,
Memories within me are enshrined.

August 2013

CHRISTMAS CARD LIST

We have an address list for Christmas cards. Each
year, we reflect on it in relation to those who have
passed on and those who we are no longer in
contact with.

Our Christmas card list gets shorter
   with each passing year.
Is it what we said or did?
   Or something not so clear?

A death or illness maybe?
   Or just the passing time?
Or postage, or enviro costs,
   that contact now defines?

Some reasons are understandable,
   some we do not know.
Perhaps they'll send one next year,
   or just one more no-show.

January 2015

People

SPRING TRAINERS

An example of people coming together with their similar skills but unique experiences and personalities is a project I ran at British Airways from 2001 to 2002 with a team of 22 contractors working through a contracting agency called *Spring*. This was helping to train British Airways staff to use their new *Amadeus* booking system.

The team was an eclectic lot from a variety of backgrounds. Some were new to contracting and some were old hands who, like me, had sourced their own work for many years. I thought, particularly, about the trainers and specialists for whom this was their first contracting role and how they would now have to find a new contracting role or go back to an employed position.

Contracting is rewarding in terms of lifestyle and remuneration, as long as one can live with the uncertainty of finding work when a contract ends.

Oh happy band of Trainers,
  now the end is nigh,
Onward you must all look,
  to where future jobs may lie.
As with all jobs and projects,
  which must have start and end,
So now we shall be parted,
  just goodbyes left to send.

Thanks for your toil and efforts,
  for all duties now complete,
Thanks for timesheets and expenses,
  and deadlines you've worked to meet.
Thanks for support where needed,
  and helpful hints and tips,
We've all gained from others' knowledge,
  all gained from many such bits.

So now the time of parting,
  so now the sad adieus,
We go our different ways,
  as all contractors do.
To new tasks and challenges,
  we must now our sinews bend,
'Til we have 'nough money,
  to say, 'This is the end!'

The message that I leave you,
  the one to comprehend,
Is learn to live with uncertainty,
  it's the contractor's lot to spend,
Those midnight hours just thinking
  until the night time ends,
'Where will the next job come from?
  'How will I pay the bills?'
'Who will want to use me —
  with my very special skills?'

Goodbye, you band of trainers,
  depart to differing ways.
Some may stay for cut-over duties,
  some will do come what may.
Life's paths may take us differing directions,
  which sometimes seem at loss,
Maybe in some future contract,
  our paths may come to cross.

2002

FRIENDSHIP

Friendship is a memory,
  friendship is a smile,
Walking arm-in-arm,
  for that extra mile.

It can be sharing laughter,
  sometimes sharing pain;
Friendship counts for so much,
  it helps to build our gain.

The things we do in friendship,
  whether small or big,
Count towards a mutual bond,
  which strengthens as we dig.

Deeper go the roots,
  stronger grow the ties.
Broader grow the branches,
  stretching far and wide.

Friendship means so much to me,
  it means so much to you.
True friendship lasts through thick and thin,
  friends - good and true.

November 2018

BEHAVIOUR

Behaviour is a complex thing,
We love, we hate, we speak, we sing.
To live we act - in many ways,
And change that act throughout our days.
Those with masks can yield surprise,
Others are without compromise.
One thing's for sure with this human play,
Our behaviours set the scene…

   …and so plough the way.

August 2015

CRINGE, CRINGE

Written when considering some of the more forgettable moments encountered during 50-odd years of alcohol consumption …

♡♡♡

Cringe, cringe after that binge,
  remember what's better forgot!

Cringe, cringe whilst others do whinge, 'bout
  your antics and foolery—
    when you cared not a jot!

The wine has flowed, the beer is sunk and you
  have shown how to live through a flunk!

And the morning brings a headache —
  and who knows what?

Time has marched on, but your embarrassment
lives on—
  and with friends, your collar is still so hot.

Cringe, cringe and remember this —
  your cringe moments are forget-me-nots!

September 2009

PRECISION AND ACCURACY

An article in *Money Management* magazine used the incorrect phrase 'life insurance' rather than the correct phrase 'life assurance'. 'Assurance' relates to life-protection products and 'insurance' refers to non–life-protection products.

Upon bringing the error to the attention of the journalist, I was informed that it is a magazine historical style note to use 'insurance' rather than 'assurance'. I pointed out that the line between precision and accuracy can be a fine one. However, in journalism, I suggested the correct use of the industry language falls on the side of being accurate—

The incorrect balance between precision and accuracy results in wasted effort and money, such as making a product that will last long after it has served its purpose. Quality management is all about delivering fitness for purpose; just like Goldilocks and the porridge – not too hot, not too cold; just right.

Recognising the difference between precision and accuracy, and knowing when to use either approach, is a key to the successful use of one's time and other resources.

The line between precision and accuracy,
Can be a fine one for some to see.
What is right for you may be wrong for me;
And reference needed to the dictionary,
Or thesaurus, to discover accuracy.

Contracts may need precision,
With legal eagles making the decision;
Finely tuned words with meaning,
Means a polished drudge — precise and
gleaming.

Journalists make do with accuracy,
If their training has helped them to see,
The link with truthful reporting,
Can help their readers with their understanding.

Precision is akin to gold plating;
Accuracy is quality — just right for making;
The right product, image or impression.
I trust this message is an object lesson…

January 2015

ESTIMATING

You will no doubt be familiar with the expression, 'I'll be with you in five minutes' or 'It's just a couple of minutes' walk'. How often do we find those few minutes extend by double, treble – or lots more?

Some popular estimating approaches I have gathered from others include:

WAG   Wild Arsed Guess

WFIA   Wet Finger In the Air

WDTWYH   What Do They Want To Hear?

DE-JDI   Don't Estimate – Just Do It

WCIGAW   What Can I Get Away With?

These approaches will be familiar to those who are engaged in project management, where a lot of estimating is really guessing — just look at project overruns on projects funded by the government.

Estimating is a skill
   that some would die for or even kill.

When making progress to an end
   our optimism will surely bend.

Any answer is acceptable
   to others with — rose-tinted spectacles.

October 2015

FINANCIAL PROCRASTINATION

Managing the family's financial affairs has become a burden of my own making and is another insight into precision and accuracy. As I have developed my investing knowledge, my research has become a never-ending task; there is so much information about the subject.

This has resulted in my collecting piles of financial tear-outs from magazines, and, as that pile has grown, I have recognised that I can never hope to re-read them. So, I began implementing a practical investment approach based on individual equities. My desire for precision has led to procrastination…

The answer is to simplify and this leads me to consider funds only and, in particular, investment trusts. Delegate the job to investment specialists.

I am drowning in information,
   leading me to procrastination.

Never one to pass a sign,
   or newspaper, book, or words designed.

To cause me to pause for thought and reflection,
   thus, from my path, I suffer deflection.

Leading me to consider,
   which way now — oh, how I dither.

Our money on standby; never moving,
   investment research still is proving,

To me, a task never-ending,
   perhaps we are better off just spending.

January 2015

DIETARY PROCRASTINATION

I have struggled with gluttony and related weight control for many years and have resolved the matter by taking purposeful exercise in the form of labouring at physical work, swimming, or walking. This approach is working for me.

We are built to fuel ourselves and then run on the savannah; it is our sedentary lifestyle that leads to our being overweight.

I will not start tomorrow,
  I didn't start today;
No matter when I don't start,
  the fat just will not go away.

At breakfast and at lunchtime,
  dinner or high tea,
With snacks 'tween such feasting,
  makes no change to me.

No matter how much I think —
  about less to fill my gut,
My resolve makes no difference —
  to consumption of our glut.

Perhaps I think too much about it,
  perhaps I need a rest;
Perhaps I'll eat just what I fancy,
  and so avoid the test...

September 2014

KIDS AND MONEY

Young people's apparent lack of control of their time and money caused me to write this poem, especially when discovering they have yet again run up debt on their credit cards and overdraft.

Time and money shortage
  not equalling budget summary,
Mean a life spent never making ends meet —
  constantly running.
Running to make up time —
  that's now lost forever,
Paying off mounting debt —
  on the never-never.

Running with rotating debt,
  spending time to manage it;
Time that's better spent investing—
  in a healthy budget.
Time and money shortage
  with its constant breathless running,
No time left for budgeting
to help with equal summing.

Remember Dickens's Micawber,
  wise words true today,
As they were so long ago
  when he was heard to say:
'20 pounds will only go so far
  and then that is the end,
Spending more than that,
  to constant debt you'll bend.'

19 pounds and 50 pence
  is the better choice;
Those extra 50 pence
  will add to help you voice:
'With no debt worries,
  I can afford to save and spend
On life's little pleasures,
  as well as kith, and kin.'

The cost of life's pleasures comes secondary
  to those of life's necessities.
Budgets help to bring them both to
  a priority for your kin and you.
Spending for tomorrow, living for today,
Leads to money misery — in every way.

January 2015

SCRAPIN' OUT THE DISH

My wife, Maureen, is an excellent cook and I
would like to think she takes it as a compliment
that I should enjoy her food so much that I cannot
resist the final scrapings of her pie dishes – crispy,
crunchy left-overs!

♡♡♡

Scrapin' out the cookin' dish
  is a pleasure few can share,
For every table of four — or six —
  only one can this delight ensnare…

Cottage pie or cauliflower cheese,
  no matter what the dish,
To scrape around the sides
  is all that I can wish.

Sex is so momentary
  and though memories may be long,
But what can beat the cookin' dish,
  where this moment's passions belong?

August 2010

PROMISES

Promises are many,
  like grains of sand and stars,
Plentiful and scattered,
  some near, some very far.
Some become reality,
  meteors shining bright,
Others end up broken,
  just a fast-fading light.

Promises are easy made,
  without a second thought,
With time to then reflect —
  on what we now have wrought.
Kept or just forgotten,
  for others to consider,
Time to offer more to,
  the next unguarded bidder.

January 2016

ECHOES

Reflections on life and lives and the interactions
between all of us.

♡♡♡

The echoes of our lives
   pass along the years,
Our living and our loving,
   our laughter and our tears.

Each ripple that we make
   travels on and on,
An interacting pattern—
   makes us all as one.

So think of this tomorrow — no —
   think of it today…
Everything we do counts —
   in each and every way.

2006

FALLEN ANGELS

Written to complement Ruheen's poem *Demons* on the *Hello Poetry* website, published as a daily selection on 28 March 2020:
https://hellopoetry.com/poem/2812310/underrated/

♡♡♡

Who are the fallen angels?
Are they demons that WE make?
By life's varied interactions,
Our constant give and take?

Some take more than others,
Those others left behind
Others who then fight for more,
Fallen angels with lost minds.

March 2020

CONFLICT

John Lennon's song *Imagine* is simply that — an imagination. Conflict comes as a part of life's package. The key is to find ways to manage it successfully — easier said than done…

Pete Seeger wrote *Where have all the flowers gone* in 1955 and it has been sung by many gifted performers, perhaps most famously by Marlene Dietrich, who performed this song in English, French, and German; French initially in 1962. Pete's song has a gentle melody with persuasive lyrics that end where they start – the seemingly never-ending and so circular journey of life and conflict.

The attack on the World Trade Center twin towers on 11 September 2001 caused me to reflect on the causes of conflict. Although my opening thoughts to this category of poem indicate that I perceive conflict as a part of life's package, perhaps it is akin to a complex set of diseases such as cancer. If so, the more we try to understand it, the better chance we have of managing it and maybe one day finding the magic-bullet cure.

HARD HEARTS, SOFT HEADS

The named places are more akin to the year of
this poem's writing.

♡♡♡

Little red robin fight if you must,
Your cause is so mighty, your cause is so just.
To die for your loved ones, for family and friends,
Means your ethos and bloodline
   will go on to the end.

The other red robin will die today,
Fighting for his cause, in his inimitable way.
Defending his loved ones, he'll lay down his life,
His passing momentary in this annual strife.

Young man in battle, young man on the streets,
With head high and mighty, the enemy to meet;
Thinking of accolades and glory and gods,
You'll make all the running and beat all the odds.

The other young man will die today,
Fighting for his cause, in his inimitable way.
Defending his causes, he'll lay down his life,
His passing momentary in this urban strife.

Tribes meet to differ as differ they must,
You don't say what I say, and what I say is just.
And so we will spill blood so my words prevail,
And so your tribe will suffer those Calgary nails.

The other tribe will die today,
Fighting for their cause, in their inimitable way.
Defending their values, they'll lay down each life,
Their passing momentary in this ongoing strife.

What could be more noble
    than courage and steel?
To wipe out those others who never could kneel
To my altar so sacred, so righteous and fine,
When all had failed, I made them toe the line.

From ancients to crusades,
    Ghengis Khan and more,
Through gypsies and Jews and 'red' Indians —
    at every shore,
The brave hearts have raped
    and plundered and slain;
Nothing to lose and everything to gain.

And so to the future down paths so well-trod,
In the twenty-first century, some still look to God,
To excuse such excesses that lead from just talk,
The road is so well-known, it's so easy to walk.

In Israel[1] and Ireland[2], New York[3] and Beijing[4],
We just keep on killing —
  is it such a wonderful thing?
The rivers of blood that Powell[5]
  spoke of so finely,
Will only happen if we do not act timely.

To value the difference, to value the (wo)man,
To build on our strengths
  and to give what we can.
To help others who need us,
  to help build such lives,
That are worthy to them
  and contribute to all hives.

From robins to tribes there will be death today.
For loves and for causes, in blood, they will pay.
The victors will dance as they take yet more life,
Another's, so pitiful, is the cost of such strife.

2001

[1] *Israeli/Palestinian conflict. ? to date.*

[2] *Irish 'Troubles'. circa 1969 to 1998.*

[3] *New York. Twin Towers attack. 2001.*

[4] *Tiananmen square massacre. 1998.*

[5] *Enoch Powell. British politician. 1968 'rivers of blood' speech. Possibly influenced by massacres occurring during the partition of India in 1947.*

IN THE NAME OF GOD

General reflections on terrorism and suicide bombers were the genesis for this poem and the wickedness which can come from imposing our will on others.

More recently, I have researched the root causes of terrorism, which is often related to unresolved injustices, and although I can sympathise with such causes, I still feel nothing can justify the slaughter of innocents in war or by terrorism.

♡♡♡

In the name of God today,
   I shall take your life away.
In God's name, but by my hand,
   I will terrorise your land.
With bombs and fire and also fear;
   my message will be so clear:
No one but I shall rule,
   especially not yours and you.

My name is bigotry,
   my style is hypocrisy.
Hate and death I bring — in God's name —
   and the prayers I sing.
Forgiveness is not for me,
   you'll live as I say — and will also die.

Conflict

None can be so right as me and my sect
   until another way is found to correct
The seeds of man's moral decline;
   it is my fate to so define
The end for you and the end for me,
   for as you die, so I am free.

Remember this, as your blood and brains
   defile the earth beneath your scattered remains,
In the name of God is how I act,
   and with me — you will — join that pact!

July 2009

AFGHANISTAN – THE PRICE

I wrote *The Price* in September 2009. At the time there was fierce fighting in Helmand, and indeed, a year earlier a colleague had lost his son there, who was in the Royal Marines (IED).

I reflected on the funding of the conflict, partly through the drug trade; I considered how, while people were generally supportive of our servicemen and women fighting in Afghanistan, they were also funding the Taliban by creating demand for drugs derived from Afghanistan's produce.

♡♡♡

I've done the nation's bidding,
　with courage and with blood.
I've found the wild fanatic,
　in Helmand's dirt and mud.
I've killed our nation's enemy,
　I've fought and faced our foes.
I've paid the price you asked me,
　that price has been my close.

Conflict

Now as you mourn me in my carriage,
  through the streets of my hometown,
As you pay those last respects,
  as the sun is going down,
Remember the bombs and bullets –
  that ripped me into shreds –
Were paid for by those who sniffed and snorted
  and smoked and cut…
    those carefree, careless dopeheads.

The produce of that far-off land,
  the redness of its flower,
The purple seeds within it,
  the sweetness and the sour,
Those seeds that funded terror,
  those seeds that blew your minds,
Those seeds that made my coffin bearers –
  the ones now left behind.

I've paid the price this summer,
  with courage and with blood,
The price for your self-served pleasure,
  soaked into Helmand's mud…

September 2009

SURVIVAL

Survival in our modern society is generally not a matter of life and death. Apart from through television news, documentaries, dramas, etc., most of us never come near ultimate survival challenges.

This is why I respect the efforts of wild animals who must daily live with the prospect of death pronounced by a predator, or more slowly from starvation, especially if wounded or old.

HARRY II

It all started over 60 years ago when Kev, a childhood pal of mine, found an injured magpie. He took it home and nurtured it back to health. After release, *Dudley*, as Kev called his feathered friend, remained a garden visitor. I recall thinking about how great it must feel to help an injured animal regain its health and faculties. Little did I know that the opportunity would present itself to me twice in the coming years.

I found Harry, a blackbird, on our lawn early one morning. He was in a state, probably from an attack by a cat. Although he looked dead, we decided to wait and see, so we left him in a cardboard box. Several hours later there were signs of life, so we offered him sustenance and placed him out of harm's way in our garage. His lasting damage was a blind eye.

Over the following weeks, he got stronger, and eventually it became clear that he needed to be released into the wild. So we duly had a 'launch' day, with food placed on the patio wall to help him on his way.

However, that was not the end of it, as he kept returning for more food! Harry had become tame. Eventually, he foraged for himself; we could always tell when Harry was in the garden, as he foraged with his head to one side, using his good eye to look for tasty morsels.

Harry found a mate and had chicks – even with his disability he still carried out his matrimonial duties by raising a family, searching for food for his offspring using his one-eyed approach!

Several years passed; Harry was gone and life returned to normal in our garden, with various types of birds bringing enjoyment to our family. Then, one day, early in the morning, I noticed a blackbird lying on the lawn. I repeated the procedure I had adopted for Harry, and again, after several weeks, he was up and about. We named this bird 'Harry II'. Harry II also had an injury – his tail had been removed during his struggle for survival. We wondered how he would manage to fly without this key part of his anatomy! However, fly he did and, as with Harry I (as the first blackbird had posthumously been named), he fathered and raised a family, feeding them in our garden. Apart from his lack of a tail, his other distinguishing mark was a fleck of white feathers.

The trials, tribulations, and ultimate successes of Harrys I and II caused me to ponder life and its challenges. Apart from the joy those two birds gave our family, they inspired me to consider how they overcame significant challenges to lead near-normal lives. This inspiration is demonstrated in a poem I consequently wrote about Harry II and his struggle to survive and prosper.

We saw other blackbirds in our garden, with the white flecks in their feathers; probably offspring. They reminded me of the Harrys and the lessons they have for all of us on our journey through life.

How fortunate for us to have had two such opportunities!

♡♡♡

Fine little blackbird without a tail,
Raising a family, you must not fail.

Others so swift
  with their feathers and plume,
'Tis you who must struggle
  to make ends meet so soon.

Your young ones need you so,
  and their lives do depend
On your hunting endeavours
  and your feeding without end.

One day they must fly
  and hunt for themselves,
With brand new fine feathers
  and fine-looking tails.

Let's hope your tail grows back
  and so once again
You can look at your fellows
  and be seen as the same.

By then all your struggles
   with aerodynamics so poor
Means you'll pass others' aerobatics
   with finesse and more.

Those earlier struggles
   will now turn to success,
Bringing you victory
   and ensure you're the best.

With all of life's battles
   'tis the struggle that builds
The character and fortitude
   to overcome ills.

The making and breaking
   of any of us depends
On bearing the hardships
   and focussing on the end.

For the dream or the vision of whatever we ask.
'Tis ours for the taking if we bend to the task.

Fine little blackbird without a tail,
Raising a family, you must not fail.

Today you inspired me to recognise this date
I have with the future to assure my fate.

July 2002

THE BIRD STILL FLIES

I was travelling home by train one evening, after
having attended an investor meeting in London,
at which a lot was said about change being driven
by technological advances.

As we crossed the north Hampshire countryside,
I observed a large solitary bird making its way
across the golden wheat fields. I reflected on how
birds had followed the same lifestyle for millions
of years, whilst our human lifestyles had changed
beyond recognition within a few hundred years.

New tech advances as old tech dies,
Yet in the air above us, the bird still flies.

Mega, mega data —
   measurement is so fine,
Building giant data banks
   on which our technology can dine.

Its fruits refine our lifestyle —
   to enhance, improve, and more,
And soon perhaps to forever close
   that last exit door.

So will we live forever,
   humans so complete?
Enhancing robotic arms and muscles —
   a life ongoing and so sweet?

That bird will die soon,
   its offspring will take its place,
Our legacy also plain to see —
   a robotic human race.

The birds still fly, sheep still graze,
   across the landscape wide;
Robots farm and replicate —
   will they ever wonder why?

May 2020

EMPTY BOWL

Upon viewing my fulsome breakfast and
comparing it with people in other continents
facing hunger and starvation.

♡♡♡

The empty bowl awaits,
  along with the empty plate,
Waiting — then filled with cereal and oats,
  plus dried fruit, followed by toast.
The empty teacup fills with coffee,
  to complete my breakfast repast,
Ready for the day's endeavours,
  with a stomach full of ballast.

The empty bowl awaits,
  along with the empty plate,
Along with empty stomach,
  with hunger the constant theme.
No cereal and oats today:
  such a feast is just a dream.

January 2020

FUND MANAGER'S PRAYER

After reading *Where Are All the Customers' Yachts?*
and some press articles about the charges that
fund managers make, along with the debate
about active vs. passive funds, and finally the fall
from grace of fund manager Neil Woodford, I
reflected on whether many successful fund
managers rely more on luck
than judgement.

Survival

O God of Mammon and money,
  please make me rich today,
Or make me rich just slowly,
  with stock selection, I pray.

Give me wit to fool investors,
  that all is due to skill,
When all I need is divine insight —
  to help me earn my fill.

Please save me from Woodford's failings;
  I don't want to take his place,
With his fund foreclosure
  and in professional disgrace.

I don't want to win the lottery —
  I just want a million or two.
Surely that's not a lot to ask for
  from someone as bountiful as you?

So let me take my place –
  with giants of our investment industry,
So investors can look with pride and envy —
  and think it is all down to me….

January 2020

PHILOSOPHY

Philosophy is defined as the study of the general and fundamental nature of reality, existence, knowledge, values, reason, mind, and language.

It is fundamental to our values; implicitly, it underpins whatever we do, no matter what religion or other approach we use to guide our lives.

This is why it gets special treatment with the mention of three guest poets.

INSPIRATION

RUDYARD KIPLING
1865–1936

Rudyard Kipling is my favourite poet —
generally easy to read, meaty subjects
and with meaning.

My book of his poems is very well worn and is
now over 50 years old.

<u>The Six Wise Men</u> is one of my favourites, albeit
its actual title is *Six Honest Serving Men*.

Those six being, What and Why and When and
How and Where and Who.

They are easy words that are the arrowheads of a
curious and questioning personality. They make
good conversation generators as long as they do
not come across as an interrogation…

The 'she' Kipling refers to in the poem is, of
course, Queen Victoria.

Also Kipling's poem "If –" is very profound and
uplifting in times of trouble.

WILLIAM BLAKE
1757 TO 1827

I particularly like the first stanza of William Blake's poem *To See a World in a Grain of Sand*. It has resonance through context by comparison — grain of sand — wild flower — infinity in the palm of your hand — eternity in an hour:

To See a World in a Grain of Sand

To see a World in a Grain of Sand

And a Heaven in a Wild Flower,

Hold Infinity in the palm of your hand

And Eternity in an hour.

ANNIE BESANT
1847–1933

Annie Bessant is a recent discovery for me. Her poem *Hidden* (which is actually called her mantra) touches deeply on the singularity of aspects of our universe and our place in it:

Hidden

Oh, hidden life, vibrant in every atom,

Oh hidden light, shining in every creature,

Oh hidden love, embracing in oneness,

May each who feels as one with these,

Know he is one with every other.

Philosophy

THE DEATH OF LOGIC & REASON

and the resulting victory of emotion

The struggle between these two drivers of our decisions was written during a philosophical moment considering the damage that revenge can do to ourselves and why forgiveness is so necessary for us to move on with our lives.

'Vengeance is mine',
  said the heart to the head,
'Completeness of my victory,
  with my near nemesis, nigh on dead.

'The arrow of my revenge
  has found its way to home,
'And the vanquished feels the pain
  right through to the bone'.

 'Forgiveness is the answer',
  said the head to the heart,
'Logic and reason should drive us
  from the very start.

'The arrow you have fired
   has surely found its mark
'For not only has it found your near nemesis,
   but it has also found me —
                — you and I now forever apart.

'For by taking your revenge,
   now all can clearly see,
'As well as your near nemesis,
   you have also killed me.'

AND THE RESULTING VICTORY OF EMOTION

'Wait! Wait!'
   cried the heart to the head,
'Don't die because
   of what I've done and said.

'Together we are strong,
   whilst alone I am so weak;
'I never would have meant for
   such havoc to wreak.

'Together, we're the soul,
   of the human we have cared,
'Apart, he is damned
   and so can never be spared.'

September 2014

IN-FIN-I-TEEEE

The conundrum of considering infinity has always (?) fascinated me! Perhaps my efforts to understand the cosmos in terms of physics and mathematics will take longer than I may have left on this mortal coil...

Why is it with infinity?
The end of which I struggle to see?
I go in loops in space and time,
Also loops within my mind.

Around in circles never-ending,
No left or right — never bending
From the path or from the curve
Set by Pi — I cannot swerve.

Following Pi without constraint,
Inside-out — the lines I paint,
Turn upside down and other ways,
Never-ending, endless days.

From constant Planck, and Boltzmann, too,
The numbers stream, too many true
For me to count, for me to see,
For me to make sense of… In-Fin-I-Teee.

May 2012

THE TASTE OF LOVE

I was inspired to write this poem upon watching the TV programme *Last Tango in Halifax,* a somewhat light-hearted drama about entangled relationships.

Love is sweet, love is short,
Love is worth the pain it brought;
Love can never be the same,
Once it's followed by the pain.

Hearts are broken, tears are shed,
Bringing respite to the head.
So now the contest can begin,
Heart and head – which shall win?

To relive moments, lost forever,
Memories, dreams, passionate endeavour.
Who can tell how this unfolds?
For each of us, the story's told.

For each us, there are two parts,
How we are ruled – by head and heart.
These two taskmasters do not see
What their rivalry does to you and me

For we must live with both these traits
And master them to master our fates.

December 2012

ACTUARIALLY...

A reflection on our lifespan, as calculated by a
nameless calculator of death using statistics –
known as the actuary.

Approaching a landmark birthday in May 2014
and realising I may have only 20 years of life left
for any further achievement.

♡♡♡

Ac – tuar – i – al – ly,

That's the way it has to be.

Three-score ten plus five or more,

Leads us to the final score.

By adding years arith – met – ic – ally,

Shows how long we have — ac-tu-ar-ially.

But by living life to the full,

Make precious memories reality.

The way we live, the way we love,

How we laugh and how we sigh,

The way we smoke and drink and eat,

The way we dance, the way we die.

Every piece and part of life,

All adds up or takes away;

Meaning more, meaning less,

Hour by hour, day by day.

Until our living catches up;
All our pleasures, all our sinning,
Come to naught when at the end,
Death's clasp is finally winning.

By our living as we wish it,
Compounded, plus or minus;
All that we could want or have,
A timeline – yet so timeless.

April 2014

LANGUAGE

Language and its use fascinates me and I am becoming more precise in my use of it, to avoid ambiguity and the related communication errors.

However, apart from a few other pedantic friends, it appears that no one is that interested. And so, under the banner of, 'language is a flexible feast that changes over time' people continue to misuse words and contribute to a new Tower of Babel.

PRO-VANITY

Upon viewing a television programme in which
there was a lot of swearing. Foul language
appears to be the norm these days — whether in
drama, comedy, or everyday life. I am culpable; a
habit picked up mainly from my days in the UK
armed forces and indeed am embarrassed when I
swear in front of others – perhaps swearing is a
form of Tourette's syndrome…

Fuck this, fuck that, even fuckin' 'ell
      — I hope they do.
French connection in UK
      — perhaps you'll be there, too.

Jesus Christ, Oh My God,
  religious meaning or maybe not?
What the fuck does the deity
  have to do with my daily lot?

Bastard, whore, or something more,
  so long as it's profane,
Cunt, prick, twat, dick,
  they all mean much the same.

A language built through a thousand years,
  its beauty and its style,
Now torn asunder with so few words,
  and thoughtless floods of bile.

2011

TAUTOLOGY

I commented to Hamish McRae, a journalist with
the *Independent* newspaper, about his use of
tautology, and he riposted that it adds cadence. It
is time for me to drop my war on tautology…

Let the English language be,
Let it grow for all to see.

Building up, building down,
    tautological traps ensnare
All but the very most language aware.

Time to let the language flow,
To live and die – to be just so.

Cadence adds meaning to the piece,
By adding (up), so does that meaning increase.

Raise the flags for common sense!
Tautology is fine – with cadence!

2011

HE HAD A FALL

The inspiration for this poem came from my lifelong friend (from the age of five), Rob, who pointed out how the patronising phrase 'had a fall' implies some form of age-related disability, and that by referring to such an event as, 'falling over', the ageist connotation is lost. Thus, we (somewhat) oldies can retain our dignity and alignment with the rest of the human race for a little bit longer…

This subtle change of phrase is pedantry with a purpose – I can see the rationale for politically-correct language!

♡♡♡

'He had a fall, poor thing', they said,
  helping him from floor to bed;
'No,' he cried, 'I'm just fine.' I just fell over —
  it was the wine'
So as we age, our identity
  is defined by others — imposed senility.
By changing words,
  with grammatical correctness,
We avoid ageing implied — by indirectness.

August 2015

PLACES

Places can have meanings for us, based on our experiences when we have been to them.

One of the most memorable places I have visited was the Outer Hebrides, as a soldier in the late 1960s. This included various tours to Hirta, the largest island in the St Kilda Archipelago. I plan to write a poem about the Hebrides, the land, the sea and the hospitable people I met there.

But in the meantime…

STRATFORD SCENES

Upon viewing the London skyline from the
Stratford Holiday Inn restaurant terrace during a
client visit.

♡♡♡

I sat out on the terrace, back towards the bar,
Taking in the landscape of city, planes, and stars.

With dinner from the ocean,
   calamari and sea bream,
With buildings in the distance,
   a panoramic scene.

The trains pass by below me,
   on their busy way,
With commuters and relaxers,
   from and to their busy days.

A great city in the distance,
   Canary Wharf, Millennium Dome,
And crane still building structures,
   but not so far from home.

Stratford International Station,
   a new metropole of esteem,
New town, new thoughts, new views —
   a brand new world it seems.

August 2014

POEMS FOR PARKS

Our parks and open spaces are a blessing; they are places to get away from the bustle of life. These three short poems are dedicated to those who have the foresight and will to ensure such vital organs of our society are kept for us to enjoy.

♡♡♡

Sit for a while at this place,

Watch the children play a while.

Look at the trees and open space,

Enjoy the scene — enjoy your smile!

♡♡♡

Come here to enjoy the play,

Just a moment — or why not stay?

While away your precious time,

Your rest-of-day will be just fine.

♡♡♡

Litter, litter everywhere
  instead of in the bin,

Why do we drop our bags and stuff —
  what causes this great sin?

Where is the pain in using
  that well-provided receptacle?

Who will join me in making our parks —
  a little more respectable?

August 2011

NOSTALGIA – WHERE NEXT?

Nostalgia is a far-off land —
   silver clouds, no shifting sands.
A place where once, all was well,
   far better than the current hell.
The past is reality — it does not change,
   we can let it be.
The future is ours to shape,
   to craft that future — what will you make?

December 2018

ENVIRONMENT

People worry about carbon and global warming and, of course, we should be concerned. However, it is becoming clear that the bigger threat is the broader one to our environment. If we should become self-sustaining in relation to energy, then will this mean we produce even more stuff which is then disposed of into our environment? And what would such unconstrained consumption mean to the natural resources we have?

INSPIRATION

P. F. SLOAN

P. F. Sloan was very successful during the mid-1960s, writing, performing, and producing hits for artists such as Barry McGuire, The Searchers, Jan and Dean, Herman's Hermits, Johnny Rivers, The Grass Roots, and The Mamas & the Papas.

His song *Eve of Destruction* is a protest song written in 1965. And I particularly recall its recording by Barry McGuire. A very powerful rendering of a very powerful message.

Although mainly about war, the song has a resonance today, in relation to the environment as well as the increasingly dangerous geopolitical situation we face in this early part of the 21st century.

It's on YouTube — I recommend listening to it.

ALBERT HAMMOND

Albert Hammond has written many songs such as *Free Electric Band*, *It Never Rains In Southern California*, and *The Air That I Breathe*, and for many artists.

My favourite is *Down By The River*, one of the first environmental songs. As with *Eve of Destruction*, it is probably timelier today, than when it was first released in the 1960s.

I was fortunate enough to see Albert perform live in the summer of 2015 when he toured the UK and Europe. At 70 he was still a powerful and captivating performer with much originality.

POOR PLASTIC BAG

I have never understood why people drop litter
rather than take it home. I wonder what their
homes are like: Are they pristine, or are they the
mess that littering indicates?

Poor plastic bag,
   blowin' in the wind,
Not the answer
   'bout which Bob Dylan sings.
Sucked from Mother Earth,
   processed and refined,
By-product of ethylene
   used to carry out our dines.

Poor plastic bag used and abused,
Left to desecrate and disintegrate,
A fate no one would choose.

Some bags get reprocessed,
   environmentally friendly;
Other bags become —
   our environmental enemy,
Destined to forever roam
   till exhausted and torn,
Hung from a branch forlornly,
   our landscape to adorn.

Poor plastic bag,
  sinned against and abused,
Blowin' cross the landscape
  ne'er again to be used.
Whate'er your future holds, be bold,
  blow on toward your end,
For your return to Mother Earth,
  is where we will you send.

Tesco and Sainsbury brothers
  have all met kinder fates,
Reused as doggy poo bags
  or joined the recycling wait.
Why is it we drop you
  as if you're never owned?
What have you done to deserve this fate,
  discarded and alone?

September 2009

DORSET WEATHER

Reflections on a very wet spring 2012 and my
wife, Maureen's, first attempt at growing
runner beans.

♡♡♡

Garden lawn is water-logged,
   though sun shines brightly — why?
How has yesterday's deluge
   now turned into clear blue sky?

April–May transition passed —
   happened overnight,
Fairy wand was waved —
   taking us from dull to bright.

Maureen's runner beans climbing,
   in sun lounge, facing west,
Waiting for planting,
   once wind and rain have given best.

A contradictory spring-time,
   a difference so extreme,
I wonder what summer holds for us,
   a nightmare or a dream?

May 2012

MOUNTAIN ASH

For years the mountain-ash tree in our garden has been overshadowed by our monstrous willow. The recent heavy pruning of the willow has, hopefully, given the mountain ash an opportunity to thrive.

♡♡♡

Mountain ash, oh mountain ash,
  shaded by the mighty willow.
Where do you find the strength to grow,
  when you're the underfellow?

Bark is cracked and growth is slowed
  by that mighty monster next door.
Is there a magic mixture
  to bring you to the fore?

Like the hare and tortoise racing,
  you will find there is a way,
So you can rise above it tomorrow
  – if not today.

And then your time will come,
  to stand and tell your story.
Mountain ash and willow too –
  embraced in natural glory.

September 2013

PUBLIC SERVICE CORRUPTION

The public sector is the part of an economy that is controlled by the state and, in the UK, it employs just over a sixth of working people – over five million people compared to the private sector's 26 million plus.

Most people who work in the public service, be they central or local government service, teachers, police, fire brigade, judiciary, health workers, armed forces etc., are no doubt honest and hard-working individuals and good team players.

Recent press reports about various individual and institutional failings indicate that all is not right with various aspects of our public services, such as our NHS (Stafford Hospital), the Crown Prosecution Service (attempted rape trials), the police (Hillsborough disaster enquiry), and the Post Office IT scandal in which sub-postmasters were treated terribly.

My own experiences since 2013 indicate there is a systemic aspect to the malfeasance and corruption at work in our public service.

A CLEAR NIGHT THIS MORNING

I woke up very early and got up for a cup of tea. From the window, I saw the total clarity and, so, the beauty of the night sky. This caused me to consider how I was gaining clarity in relation to my voluntary role at a local NHS Hospital, where my desire for honesty and openness was met with unbelievable resistance from senior managers and governors; and how these events can be used to bring about better governance across the UK's NHS.

Developing a sense of purpose when faced with adversity helps one to develop the strength to see things through.

♡♡♡

It's a clear night this morning,
  as I look up to the sky.
A clear day is dawning,
  as insights to my eye.
A billion stars are shining,
  lighting up the void,
With insights to its history,
  a story now enjoyed.

It is a clear night this morning,
  as I look into my mind.
A clear day is dawning,
  as my deepest thoughts unwind.
A thousand threads of thinking
  lighten up my load.
I have insights to the future,
  a clear and solid road.

October 2013

THE WHISTLE-BLOWER

After my removal as a governor at a local hospital in November 2013 — for asking too many of the 'right' questions — I decided to focus on improving governance by requesting Mr Jeremy Hunt, the Secretary of State for Health, to look into 13 specific points for improving the role of governors at NHS hospitals.

My efforts were met with bland responses from two under-secretaries of state and from NHS England. So I realised there was a bigger issue surrounding NHS policy and governance; mooted public engagement was, in fact, a fig leaf.

Since then, my naivety in relation to the openness of NHS managers and politicians has become more apparent, for example, with the case of Sharmila Chowdhury, a radiologist.

Sharmila worked at a London hospital, running a department of about 60 people. She whistle-blew on two doctors who were moonlighting with private work when they were on duty at the hospital. In counter-allegations, she was then falsely accused of fraud. There was no evidence of any wrongdoing on her part but plenty of documented evidence regarding the moonlighting doctors. Despite this, she was escorted out of the hospital in front of her staff.

Sharmila reported the matter to NHS counter-fraud several times along with supporting evidence and escalated the issue up the hospital management chain. She won interim relief hearing in court as well at a hospital internal appeal hearing, and the hospital management apologised for their treatment of her for raised concerns, but refused to re-employ her, stating that her role had 'become redundant'.

The two consultants continued to work at the hospital, as did the senior management who were involved.

She even met Jeremy Hunt along with other whistle-blowers but to no avail. Sharmila has been refused employment by other NHS organisations.

She has spoken with other staff at the hospital, and their views were that the hospital had not taken action against the two doctors because other surgeons may be similarly moonlighting.

The extent to which moonlighting practices are common across the NHS is an unanswered question.

It struck me that there is a deeper corruption within the NHS and that lots of people are likely to know it is going on; like the blind eye that has been turned to child/mental-patient abuse (Jimmy Savile, etc.) within organisations.

Such matters have been a revelation to me and helped me recognise how naïve I have been about governance, ethics, and basic human values within our country.

Brave souls such as Sharmila take up the fight to clear away the fudge, and so shine a light into darkest corners which are hidden by incompetent

and corrupt hospital managers, aided and abetted
by their power to spend public funds on lawyers.

♡♡♡

Who are these people
  who think that they can be
Above the Law, but out of sight —
  below where we can see?
Skulking on their daily rounds,
  with fraud and lies within them,
A creeping sore is what they are,
  gnawing at our society.

Do they act to fill some need?
Or are their wants driven by greed?
Perhaps it's the ego driven— by envy —
  of their peers,
Or maybe too-large mortgages
  and so those payment arrears.

How different they are,
  from the patients that they serve,
So privileged with separate values,
  and to have the nerve
To act against the published culture,
Shiny on top —
  but underneath behaving like vultures.

December 2015

SILENCE

Written as my contribution to the Wimborne
Speakeasy monthly meeting of writers and poets;
taking into account my experience and learnings
since 2013 of how the Establishment and public
authorities often behave when faced with
uncomfortable truths about aspects of
their behaviours.

♡♡♡

Silence can be peace;
  it can be a prayer;
It can mean us asking,
  'Is there anyone there?'

Silence can mean a gag,
  applied with physical force;
Or made through legal pressure,
  so whistle-blowers change course.

Silence can be a means,
  to indicate agreement,
Or to hide one's fear,
  a mind now filled with cement.

Less is more, or so we're told,
  by those we are beholden;
To what extent or otherwise is —
silence — golden?

February 2020

HYPOCR-I-SEE

Hypocrisy is to me

A means and way for some to see

How our actions do not meet our words,

And so that others can observe

Why those actions that we take

Cannot match the words we make,

How what we say and do have difference,

Showing the world our total ignorance,

Why is it that we cannot see

How our lives are twisted by hypocrisy?

January 2019

THE REST

Here is a miscellany, none of which seem to fit into the categories I have chosen for my other poems.

INSPIRATION: J. B. S. HALDANE

5th November 1892 – 1st December 1964

John Burdon Sanderson Haldane was a British naturalised Indian scientist; a polymath, with works in physiology, genetics, and evolutionary biology, as well as innovative contributions to statistics and biometry.

His epic and funny poem *Cancer's A Funny Thing* was written shortly before his death from cancer, while in hospital, mocking his own incurable disease, and it marks the consistent irreverence with which he lived.

http://nsmn1.uh.edu/dgraur/Texts/Cancerhaldane.htm

CREATIVITY

This poem, written from inspiration,
Helps with my mental constipation.
Helping me to think things through,
With an outcome — overdue.

So my output has become,
This short rhyme – not from my bum…

November 2017

The Rest

MA BH AIN'T SQUARE

Prostate cancer led to a radical prostatectomy for me in 2005. I noted that after curries and beer evenings, number twos had a certain 'ballistic characteristic'. Perhaps an unfair joke-dig at the expense of the excellent surgeon, Mr Wedderburn, who saved my life; I do hope he will forgive me and see the funny side of my predicament.

By 2015, I noted that trajectory was improved, so I guess my guts had finally adjusted, and so strictly speaking the poem should be in the past tense!

The wonders of modern medicine have meant that I have survived cancer, and the demise of J. B. S. Haldane in 1964 indicates how far medicine has progressed in 40-odd years.

In my case, the relatively early recognition of the symptoms and the ensuing diagnosis played a clear part; my thanks to my very alert G.P. at that time, Dr Mark Taylor.

Ma bum hole ain't squa
   even when there's really nuthin' there.
The shite squirts out
   to the left and roundabout.
Ma belly is misshapen
   with a left-handed pattern,
And ma willy has left bias —
   more than trouser hang per dias.

It ain't round either — kinda strange —
   don't ask me whya.
Ask the surgeon who did the cuts —
   and maybe ask him what the f**k?
Maybe it's a style thing for medics —
   a post-prostatectomy muck?
A private joke for every patient —
   only visible in the toilet basin!

September 2009

THE PRESENT

This present — a gift from me to you —
Will help you with what you want to do.
Be it sport or work or something else,
I'm sure of its value to yourself.
Be it for pleasure or help with pain,
It will help you with some sort of gain.

RESPONSE…

This present — a gift from you to me —
Is not what I expected it to be.
It is not what I choose or desire;
It will not set my world on fire.
Thank you for your consideration,
A gift akin to constipation…

November 2017

I WANT TO GET YOUR POETRY BOOK

I wanted to buy Roger Turner's poetry book *The Hippo* but could not find it online. I contacted Roger and he guided me to where I could get it.

♡♡♡

I want to get your poetry book
   but cannot find it online.
I'm happy to pay the eight pounds
   and to spare the time
To read all 60 poems,
   to give them all my thoughts,
But I cannot do this as things stand,
   so my desire comes to nought…

January 2020

MY PET SLUG

Upon seeing a gigantic slug crawling across our footpath and recognising it had been alive a long (slug) time to grow to that size…and was it really hurting anyone with its existence?

Leopard slugs are the gardener's friend.

♡♡♡

My pet slug is —
   as HUGE as he can be,
And I'm his only friend
   as both he and I can see.
I think he really loves me:
   he never runs away;
He's always there to greet me,
   especially on rainy days.

May 2021

YORKIE-BAR COMPETITION

Nestlé ran a competition relating to codes printed on the wrapper of their Yorkie bars. I could not read the code in mine, maybe because of the print colour. I sent the wrapper to Nestlé at 'Freepost Nestlé UK Consumer Services' (i.e., no town or postcode), as this was the new-style freepost address provided by Royal Mail and does not have a postcode.

♡♡♡

No number in my Yorkie! Oh, whatever can I do?
No prize for me to win now —
   it makes me feel so blue…
The bar itself was wondrous,
   an interim repast,
Lasting me 'til lunchtime,
   then wifey's sarnies here at last!

The address is incomplete, oh,
   where shall send my wrapper to?
Where will it end up going,
   maybe Timbuctoo?
Aha! I have the answer:
   website tells me where,
With postcode, road, and city,
   I hope it finds you there!

July 2015

DOUBLE KNOT

After double-knotting both loops and tails for 60
years or so, when tying my shoelaces, it was by
observing Leon, our grandson double-knot just
the loops and then trying this myself that I
discovered this method was easier to do and
easier to undo… So the youth of today can teach
us more than just how to use technology!

♡♡♡

To tie a double knot is something I can do,
When ensuring my lace is —
   tight upon my shoe.

Now watching grandson tie one,
   I see I was wrong,
In tying tails and bows
   the knot was over strong.

By doubling only knots not tails,
   a simpler thing to do,
Double knots are quicker tied —
   and easier to undo.

Training and observing are the stuff
   of how we improve.
With something new each day
   toward a fuller life we move.

August 2015

MY MEMORY

Last week I used your name…
Then I called you "mate."

Yesterday I called you "sir";
Today you're just a blur.

Tomorrow?
Who knows what I'll call you then or after…

May 2021

MY PET SCAB

My blooded knee was not painful,
   but the ladder left its mark,
A great big hole AND a gash,
   a wound that was so fresh and stark.

The healing was soon work in progress,
   helped by plasters and cream.
Before too long things looked up;
   nature's repair had worked, it seemed.

The scab was big and with a long bit,
   from hole down to the gash,
And as it hardened and flaked,
   patience was just too much to ask.

Pick a bit, smooth it back —
   'You don't want scars', as my Mum once said.
But what the hell it's just my knee —
   will not matter when I'm dead.

It's not the scarring or the bleeding
   stopping me from peeling it away;
It's thinking it's a part of me,
   and so should hang around a further day.

At last, it's gone — bit by bit,
   with my knee now safe and sound.
I said goodbye with the last picked off,
   back to nature in the ground.

May 2020

HELP ME PUBLISH (PLEASE...)

After unsuccessfully entering poetry competitions
as the route to publishing mine, I read Matt
Abbot's in his brilliant *Hurricane In My Head* and
decided to approach him for his help in finding
a publisher.

I've read your poetry and it's great,
   so now I aim for a similar fate.
I've written 60 poems
   and it's taken 20 years,
And now I'm in my dotage
   (actually only 71 years).
It's time to get them published
   and overcome my shyness fears.
Each poem tells a story
   to which you will relate,
A part of life you will recall —
   a part you love or hate.
So now do me a favour please
   and help me with this quest,
To find a suitable publisher
   and get these 60 off my chest.
I thank you in advance
   for I know you will suppose
my poetry is wonderful and says —
   what cannot be said with prose.
Your poems have inspired me
   for this next step in my lifelong journey,
to enhance our human insights
   before I end up on a gurney!

August 2019

WAITING FOR THE PHONE TO RING

Many are confronted by unrequited love,
especially during our youth. This is my tale from
over half a century ago.

♡♡♡

Waiting for the phone ring,
  with just one simple song to sing,
A song of love and of joy,
  one of happiness unalloyed.

When that song is sung it seems,
  my thoughts and feelings are just dreams,
The love, the joy, the happiness,
  in the depth of the abyss.

All that's left for me to sing
Is — waiting for the phone to ring.

November 2014

GOODBYE

No tale about unrequited love can be complete
without the pathos.

♡♡♡

I stood on the ship's deck
   as we waved goodbye.
You stood on the quayside
   and started to cry.

Turning your back to me —
   a puzzle unsolved…
I should have known then
   of another involved.

That was our last meet — and your love was a lie.

May 2020

GALACTIC SATNAV

I have resisted satellite navigation for many years, relying on my ability to plan journeys and actually read maps, my philosophy being to use technology when there is a need, and not just because it's fashionable.

This changed when my good friend Stuart offered me his 'TomTom' as he was getting a more up-to-date model. When he explained that it had saved him money in speeding fines, as it warned him of speed limits and speed camera locations, my financial case for having one became obvious, as I had just paid £110 to attend a Dorset 'Driver Awareness' course rather than get three points on my driving licence.

Initial experimentation using my 'TomTom' caused me to reflect where such technology could end up, especially with the possibility of private 'space cars' in the years ahead. When coupled with my imagination, this poem emerged.

Alpha Centauri,
  you're not too far away;
With galactic satnav,
  I will reach you come what may.

Travelling at light speed,
  four years is not so long,
Time enough to write this ode,
  or turn it into song.

Travelling on and outwards,
  through our Milky Way,
Our Earth left far behind me,
  I'll need a place to stay.

Something I've forgotten,
  just as I pass our Sun —
I only have my start point —
  at BH21!

February 2019

POSTSCRIPT

For many years, I have considered that our children's children may be the last generation who have to die. Medical advances cause me to consider that I may have been a pessimist and chosen immortality may be closer than we realise.

It is fitting that my final poems deal with our mortality.

In the meantime, perhaps Mr Sunderman's work ethos may be the key to longevity, and so these are dedicated to Mr Sunderman's memory.

INSPIRATION: WILLIAM SUNDERMAN

23rd October 1898 – 9th March 2003

Dedicated to William Sunderman — died aged 104 — a portent to the future.

I started writing this poem in about 2003 and rediscovered my handwritten notes in 2009. I also found the *Economist* obituary (20th March 2003) for Mr Sunderman, which inspired me to complete the poem.

When William Sunderman turned 100 he was named by the United States Congress as the oldest person in the country still at work. He was putting in an eight-hour day editing articles for a medical journal. For a break, he liked to take a turn on an exercise bicycle.

MORATOR-I-UM

Correctly forecasting that I would live beyond
2018…

♡♡♡

As I reach this mortal pass,
  an eternal place is all I ask;
A message suffice to show the ways
  I've lived my life and spent my days.

So what can be said about this life,
  with its share of work and play and strife?
What has it meant so much to share
  with you, the reader, my soul laid bare?

From start to end my time I've lent;
  it's peoples' needs to which I've bent.
To serve my fellows and myself,
  ensuring all can share the wealth…

Of knowledge, learning, kindness, and more,
   this is how I've kept my score.
And now the tally has been made,
   all in the light — not in the shade.

Compounding theory adds so much, but —
   what height does — that sum touch?
I think it's little — but that's enough;
   it's on the right side — adding up.

The sum of all has been added to,
   by seventy years of life, or so…

November 2009

TIMETABLE TO HEAVEN

Half-past six—
   time to count life's varied kicks and tricks.
Half-past seven —
   almost time to go to heaven.
Half-past eight —
   will I get past those pearly gates?
Half-past nine —
   St Peter says I'm doing fine.

October 2015

WHERE ARE YOU?

To our dead relatives and friends.

♡♡♡

Where are you?

Are you someplace far away?
Will you come back — will you stay?

Is it better than the place I'm in?
Is it really free of vice and sin?

Will I get there — will I meet you?
Will St Peter greet me too?

Will I spend time in purgatory,
My sins made visible for all to see?

Will data protection provide the clothes
For my embarrassment to not be disclosed?

Or will I be damned into perdition,
Eternal pain with no remission?

Will I find you on these paths?
Less of these thoughts,
    I'll get out of the bath!

April 2019

THINGS BETTER LEFT BEHIND

Like the entertainer's comeback, so after writing
'Morator-I-um' I reflected on two of its lines:

'And now the tally has been made

'All in the light — none in the shade'

and wrote 'Things Better Left Behind'.

For those who are curious, those things I leave
behind are not heinous.

♡♡♡

Some things are better left behind us
  after we depart,
No record for the future,
  no memories of the heart.

Things better left unsaid,
  even after we are dead.

Matters of our private lives,
  matters best forgotten,
Matters from our heart of hearts
  shared with sometimes others —
      now left to never blossom.

September 2018

How infinitesimal is the importance of anything I do, but how infinitely important is that I should do it.

Voltaire